HOW TO MEET
YOUR SOULMATE

HOW TO MEET YOUR SOULMATE

GUIDE TO MEETING THE ONE AND STARTING
A HAPPY RELATIONSHIP

HANIEH

To order additional copies of this book, contact:
Xlibris
AU TFN: 1 800 844 927 (Toll Free inside Australia)
AU Local: 0283 108 187 (+61 2 8310 8187 from outside Australia)
www.Xlibris.com.au
Orders@Xlibris.com.au
815006

CONTENTS

INTRODUCTION

For many years, I longed to be married. I wanted to be with someone who loved me and love them in return. Living in a foreign country, with no family or friends, I was alone and depressed. And although I longed for love, I didn't trust myself to love—no one else in my family had a happy relationship, and I was sure I would follow in their footsteps. I had dreams about my ideal man and relationship but didn't know how I could make these dreams reality. I asked others who had good relationships about how they met their spouses, but no one had a clue. "It just happened, we just met!"—that was the answer they all gave me. But how did they manage to be so fortunate in their early 20s when I hadn't got a single chance to meet the one for me even in my 30s? Not fair! It couldn't be true—it couldn't be just luck. I didn't want to be patient until the end of time, hoping that one day, it would happen.

I started poring over books on relationships, but they were all about what you do and don't do after you meet someone. I prayed a lot but it didn't seem to be working. The only things I had were money and a dream so I did everything I could: I got a few coaches, read many books, met amazing people along the way, and practiced what I learned. Some of this was helpful and some, not really.

Today, I am very, very happily married to the man of my dreams and this book is all about how it finally worked: the plan. It talks about everything I should have been doing much earlier to meet him. This book offers practical advice and includes simple practice exercises I have learned and practiced on my journey. Hopefully, before you know it, you will fulfill your heart's desire and start a happy, beautiful relationship and a lovely family. My earnest wish is that, with this book, you will find a path to joy and happiness.

What to expect

For me, the process I am writing about in this book took a few years. For my husband, with a different background and different attitude and with someone telling him what to do, it took only a few days to meet me. Your will take a lot less than me as you have this book. I don't know your background and your challenges, and I don't know your starting point. You might be able to smoothly go through this book and do the exercises or it might take you a few months to pass one stage and finish one chapter. Regardless of your situation, this book will guide you through meeting someone special for you.

I want this book to be very practical, so I have kept the explanations short and included effective exercises for you to do and get the result you are looking for.

ACKNOWLEDGMENT

Thanks to all my coaches and great people who helped me when I needed them the most, whether through great content they created or direct coaching.

Special thanks to Mat Boggs, Ray Behan, Melody Fletcher, John Assraf, Tony Robbins, Richard Dotts, Sara Blakely, Rhonda Byrneand, and many others.

A very special thanks to my beloved husband for his encouragement and support for writing this book.

STEP 1

The past is in the past

Today, you need to let go of the past, let go of the past relationship, let go of stories of the past you keep telling yourself, let go of blames and complaints about your childhood, and let go of people who had bad influence in your life. You need to let go of all excuses for being single. Today is the day you take control of your life and become responsible for the experiences you will have.

There are people who might have broken your heart in the past. There are people who might have told you that you are not smart, not beautiful, not good, and other negative judgements that they made about you. You have had experiences in your life that hurt. There are circumstances you don't know the way out of at this point.

Maybe you can't trust yourself and your choices anymore, maybe you are not sure if you deserve it, if you can have it, if you can keep it. You might have lots of "what if" statements in your head. That's okay, that was my starting point as well.

Let's start from me four years ago, this is how I was thinking about me: I am 29 and still single, I recently migrated from a developing country that does not have a good reputation in the media. I am an introvert with not much skill in making friends and relationships and English is not my first language, so I miss or don't understand many things in a conversation. Not very beautiful or attractive and I am fat. Most of my friends are single and they are even older than me. I don't have support from my family when it comes to marriage. Many of my family members are single or divorced. From the guys I knew in the past, they wanted something from me. I had a benefit for them and that's why we were friends at all. I don't have any role models or anyone that I know whose relationship I like and don't want to experience the same as my parents or other family members.

But, the pain of being and staying single was more than all the excuses and stories in my head. There was only one way to have what I wanted, and that was, to be committed to find the way. I tried many methods and read many materials. Here, I give you the best ones that worked.

Now let's start with finding the way out of it:

Let's start from people in your life that keep pulling you back. You might have unresolved relationships or pain from past relationships. What is important is to change the story you tell yourself. I want you to pick one person at the time and do two exercises as follows. Choose someone that you are still thinking about and not happy with because of what happened through your relationship with that person. It can be your parents or siblings, a friend, or your ex.

Exercise 1: The purpose of this exercise is well explained in this quote from Buddha, *"Holding on to anger is like grasping a hot coal with the intent of throwing it at someone else; you are the one who gets burned"*. You need to release the negative energy that pulls you back and replace it with the healing of positive energy. This way, you will be in a healthy state to meet your soulmate. You need to set yourself free and get ready for a great future.

Think about that person; there is a reason s/he was in your life, s/he has some good qualities that you know, but no one is perfect and all of us make mistakes. For now, I want you to write 10 good qualities of that person or things s/he have done for you and be thankful for them.

Person's name:

1. Thanks *Name* for ....…...…..............................…....
2. I really like the way you ....….............…..
3. I respect ....…...….............…................
4. I love the way you.........…......…......................................
5. Glad.................................…..
6. ....…...….............................…...............
7. ....…...…...........................…...............
8. ....…...….....................…...….................
9. ....…...…......................…...…..............
10. ....…...….............................…...................…........

Now is the time to forgive that person and wish that person all the best. Take a moment, close your eyes, put your hand on your heart and send your love to that person; wish them all the best.

That was it!! Congratulations! You are now one big step closer to achieving your goal of future happiness and wellbeing! You can do this exercise for as many people as needed.

Sometimes, after doing this exercise you might receive a phone call or a message from that person. It is up to you how you want to proceed. My suggestion is, read the next chapters for clarity on what to do; especially if that person is your ex and is now asking to come back to your life.

Exercise 2:

No more blame on why he/she did that to me. It might be something that happened in past that had a bad effect on you and your confidence today. You forgave the person and wished them all the best but are still not so sure if you can forget that event; you might still feel sorry for yourself for what you had to go through. Let's look at the story between you and that person from a different angle.

Think about an event in that relationship with that person, think about a mistake or something YOU did that wasn't ethically right. For example, cheating; spending his/her money without telling; talking behind his/her back, or making fun of her/him in a family gathering. Take a scenario of what YOU did that YOU are not happy about or when YOU did something regrettable that might have hurt the other person.

Here is an example:

Write where it was: *my birthday at our place, London*
Write when it happened: *mid May 2012*

Write what exactly happened: It was my birthday and he was in financial difficulty that month due to change of his job. He bought me a handbag as a gift and my friend John also asked me out and gave me a very expensive gift. The next day, I showed him what John gave me and told him he knows me better than you and I really love his gift. I also said I don't like that handbag and want to go to exchange it with something else. He looked at me and said I'm sorry to let you down.

Write what was the consequence: a few weeks later I found out he is texting a girl and going out with her.

Person's Name:...

Where it was: ....

When it happened: ....

What exactly happened:

....

....

....

....

What was the consequence:

....

....

....

Write as many as you can until the feeling of blaming that person disappears and you are no more a victim.

Depending on your circumstances and the story you are telling yourself, you might have difficulty remembering anything at all in relation to that person. You might think you did everything right in with that person. In this case, start from something else that you know wasn't good and that might be related to other people and different aspects of life. Let's say you said something not so nice to your sister and the relationship has been broken since then or you took something from work which you shouldn't have, or anything that you now know was against your ethics. Write about this the format I gave you and remember not to judge yourself, just keep writing. Afterwards, you might even remember an incident from childhood—write it down. In this manner, keep writing incidents as they come to your mind and soon you might remember something about the person that you couldn't at the beginning.

The more you can write the better. I took three weeks and wrote everything I could possibly remember in my life that wasn't my best and wasn't right according to my ethics. It was amazing how I changed after doing this exercise. I was a different person, very happy, and healthier and not a victim of life anymore.

STEP 2

The shortest path to what you want

On one occasion, I talked to a coach. I talked about being lonely for a long time and not having a relationship. I said I was happy to pay any amount to get some coaching sessions to help me on finding the one for me. He said the person you are looking for is the one you see in the mirror. He was right. The person in the mirror never let me down; she always helped me, did her best for me, protected me, and solved my problems. It was at this moment I realized that I had to be the first person I trusted, the first person I could count on.

In this chapter, I want to talk about your relationship with yourself. The best relationship starts from your relationship with you and how you treat yourself. It is important to do your best for you before someone else does it for you. If you are not taking good care of yourself and not treating yourself well, then how is it possible for someone else to do a better job for you? How should they know how to treat you well when even you don't know that? You need to create a good relationship with yourself first and then it would be easier for others who come into your life to see you as an example for treating you well. So here is an exercise to help you get started on building a great relationship with yourself; face yourself! What you will do from now on is stand in front of the mirror every day and say, "I love you". Look into your eyes and say, "I love you." When I first tried to do this exercise and looked into my eyes, the person in the mirror was upset and angry at me. I asked myself, "why?" and she said because you do nothing for me. The person in the mirror did not seem convinced; she seemed to be thinking that I was just saying the words without really meaning them; she was right. I wanted to do many things but didn't want to do things alone, I was waiting for someone special to do things together. I didn't have fun in my life. The next day again I said, "I love you" and again saw the upset me in the mirror. I said, "What can I do for you to show my love for you?", she said, show me some love, take me for some fun, maybe take me surfing. I did what she said and started feeling better about myself. Then she asked me not to be tight on myself and spend some of my income to have things that make me happy. As I kept listening to woman in my mirror, it was much easier to look into my eyes when I said I love you. I was happier, the one I faced in the mirror also was happy and grateful; my love for me was now more real. No wonder I was complaining about not having true love before. I didn't even know how to show true love to myself before this exercise! This marked a big step such that I was beginning to have a better relationship with myself and consequently, a better life. You will be surprised how many people I know met their loved one while doing something they had fun with or something they loved. So, starting today, stand in front of the mirror every and say I love you. Face yourself and you will be amazed with the result.

Something else that I need to touch on here is the shortest path to what you want; happiness is the shortest. The collective mind, the universe, the god are the ones who know all. They know what you want and how to have it. As you ask for something, you will be answered and the answer is doing what gives you true happiness at that moment. Follow the path of happiness and things will happen faster than you can imagine. Always listen to your heart; it will take you where you really want to be in life. I met my husband when I went for a tennis meetup. I really wanted to learn tennis and decided to join the group. I met him on the first day which was his second time in that group. So, check with yourself and your heart on what makes you happy and take action.

Make sure you do all the exercises explained in the last three chapters as they will define the quality of your future love life and relationship. Don't worry about doing them fast; just do them until you feel good and happy.

STEP 3

What you really want

Now after doing the previous exercises, letting go of the past and making your present life happier, it is time to design your future. Time to think about your ideal life, your ideal partner. I want you to take a moment and think about what you want in another person. And, what are your qualities that you bring with you in a relationship? How do you want to feel in your future relationship? Put on some relaxing music or a meditation track[1] and in a very calm state, think about those questions; don't over think, but get some ideas. Now write down everything you want in another person, don't be afraid to be specific. I want you to write these qualities from heart. What is your heart's desire?

Try writing 20 or more qualities you want. Then read it and see if you are satisfied with it. Give yourself some time. After maybe a few hours or a few days, write another list. Write it from your heart, read it again. Repeat this exercise a few times until your list no longer changes and is stable no matter how many times you write it. This is the list you want

---

[1]   The meditation I used to listen: https://youtu.be/2kAlgPewWgE

to keep. Once it becomes stable, you know it's the one. You might even find yourself getting emotional, you might even cry, as you see, for the first time, your heart's true desire written on a piece of paper.

The reason you need to write it a few times until it is stable and nothing is changing anymore is that the first time you might have some ego when writing qualities and they might not fully come from the heart. But as you repeat the exercise and it becomes stable, you will know it's the one. In my first list, I was writing things like highly educated and being a businessman, but what I really wanted in my heart was someone who understands me and supports me for doing my PhD later on as well as someone who has a business mindset and runs his own business because I wanted to have my own company later on. Having such a person with me would help me in my journey. So, it is important to get clarity from your heart. Spend some time on this list and take it seriously.

I know a lady in her 60s who did this exercise and met her partner in a few weeks. One lady used to date people through online apps and always had trouble in her relationships as she was choosing the wrong people for her; after doing this exercise, she suddenly got introduced to someone through one of her friends who was exactly the one she wanted from her list, and they married within one year. My husband did the same thing and he met me in a couple of weeks.

If it doesn't happen for you as fast, don't worry because it will eventually happen. Don't put any pressure or timeframe on yourself. Keep reading this book; there is some more work I need you to do. It didn't happen for me that fast as I needed more work on me, but it was worth it at the end. After everything, looking back, you will feel proud of yourself and what you have done.

Here is space for you to write your lists:

First list

1. ....
2. ....
3. ....
4. ....
5. ....
6. ....
7. ....
8. ....
9. ....
10. ....
11. ....
12. ....
13. ....
14. ....
15. ....
16. ....
17. ....
18. ....
19. ....
20. ....
21. ....
22. ....
23. ....
24. ....
25. ....

Second list

1. ....
2. ....
3. ....
4. ....
5. ....
6. ....
7. ....
8. ....
9. ....
10. ....
11. ....
12. ....
13. ....
14. ....
15. ....
16. ....
17. ....
18. ....
19. ....
20. ....
21. ....
22. ....
23. ....
24. ....
25. ....

Third list

1. ....
2. ....
3. ....
4. ....
5. ....
6. ....
7. ....
8. ....
9. ....
10. ....
11. ....
12. ....
13. ....
14. ....
15. ....
16. ....
17. ....
18. ....
19. ....
20. ....
21. ....
22. ....
23. ....
24. ....
25. ....

Fourth list

1. ....
2. ....
3. ....
4. ....
5. ....
6. ....
7. ....
8. ....
9. ....
10. ....
11. ....
12. ....
13. ....
14. ....
15. ....
16. ....
17. ....
18. ....
19. ....
20. ....
21. ....
22. ....
23. ....
24. ....
25. ....

STEP 4

Self-doubt

Doing the previous exercise, you created the ideal man/woman you want, everything from your heart. Some of you, when you look at your list, might start thinking whether you really deserve such a person or not. You might think how in the world would someone like that be interested in me! Or you might think, this person doesn't exist! In this chapter, I will be addressing self-doubts and how to deal with them. But, if you feel great and don't have any of the above, then you don't need to read this chapter, move on!

If you look at your list and think it is not possible that such a person exists then let's start from my list; in every list, I wrote: I wanted someone with blue/green eyes and that I would really like to marry an Australian or a European person. But I am a traditional Middle Eastern woman; there are many cultural differences between my world and the western world. I had recently moved to Australia at that time and was not very adapted to the culture. And my religion also doesn't help because if I wanted to marry my ideal man, I should have asked him to change his religion which makes it even harder and almost impossible for me to think that it might happen. And there were only two items on my list. So, looking at other items in my list I really felt nervous and thought I am setting myself up for failure or that I would need to compromise a lot to have at least someone close to what I want. My heart's desire had no information about the reality of my situation at that point. However, my heart was so right. My husband today is a born Australian and has a European background. He changed his religion and he has beautiful blue eyes! In the previous chapter, I mentioned I wanted him to have a business mindset and support me with my PhD. He ticked both these items and he has every single quality I ever wanted in my man plus so much more!

I sometimes get comments from people that they have never seen such a couple; others get amazed at our union. But my friends who have known me for a long time react differently and tell me they knew this would happen as such a person would be the right man for me.

My issue with self-doubt was my limited information about reality. My heart didn't have that limitation, but my brain had and always will have in any given situation. The coaching group I was attending at that time really helped me. I could see that every other person has these doubts in different forms. One woman thought she couldn't date someone because she was not working; she thought it would be an issue that would make guys go away. I then realized that her thinking was based on her life experiences and didn't necessarily reflect reality. I knew many guys who would not mind if their wife preferred to stay at home and not work. So, I could see how it was impossible in her mind but not in mine. This helped me understand that I don't need to trust my reasoning on things I truly want because my limited knowledge and information throughout my limited lifetime doesn't define the reality that governs the world and other people. You can go and find examples in celebrities or friends and family or even in news that what you think is not possible actually is not impossible. If it happens for someone else, it can happen for you. Just look for it with an open mind and you will find the examples.

Another form of self-doubt you might have is when you read your list and imagine that ideal person, thinking about yourself and saying but I am ….., if I want to have that person in my life then I need to become this and that. For example, you might think I am fat and need to lose weight before meeting my loved one or I need to quit smoking or I need to stop playing video games all day or I need a better job or I need to have some savings. It is good to become a better person every day and have goals, but believe that you are good just the way you are and can make someone else happy by simply being in their life.

In my case, I thought I was fat and needed to lose weight. I got a personal trainer and in the first session, he asked me my goal and how he could help me. I told him that I wanted to meet my ideal man and get married and needed to lose 10kg. So, I lost 7 kg in 3 months and after that reached my ideal weight with some diets. There I was at my ideal weight but I still had not met anyone close to my ideal man. As I started to lose hope, I started gaining weight again and training and diet weren't working anymore. Funny enough, when I met my husband, I had actually gained all that weight back. But being in the sports industry and having very good habits and a healthy lifestyle, he helped me and pushed me to be healthier and more active which was good for me.

You might think you need to change something that you really enjoy in your life, such as playing video games, to meet that person you want. But let me tell you, I know a couple that met each other through online video games in two different countries. The guy's parents provided free accommodation for them and they don't need to work much for their expenditure so they spend the majority of their time on entertainment.

Let's say you think of not having savings and your finances as a setback that will prevent you from meeting your desired girl. My husband registered for a real estate course just 3 months after we started dating and had to invest all his savings in it; 2 months later, he was forced to leave as a director and had to start looking for a job. But I was with him; we helped each other and managed to overcome these challenges and started making money in a way none of us could do alone; 6 months after that, we bought our first home and soon after, a new car and then also planned our engagement. If we had been alone, both still renting, we would not have been able to grow this fast. We would not have recovered so fast from the setbacks in our lives and couldn't have enjoyed each other's company and love. So, don't stand still and wait for everything to be perfect. What you want can be much easier and more achievable when you have someone else helping you along the way.

Another form of self-doubt can be the feeling of not deserving the best. This should not be the case if what you wrote came from your heart and if you are doing the exercises I gave you in the previous chapters. So, if that's the case you can go back to the beginning of the book and do the exercises again. When I had my list, I didn't have this book as guidance and I was getting information from different resources not knowing what was working and what wasn't. As a result, that time I just couldn't trust myself and wait for things to happen. What I did was compromise; I started searching for a similar person, a person who still shares the same culture and belief as me and colorful eyes would be a bonus. I met one man after another and got into more self-doubt; I couldn't trust myself anymore because it wasn't working. It was like lying to myself and whoever I was meeting. I wasn't satisfied. As they weren't the right people for me, they couldn't see my values; they put me down and made me feel unworthy. I was setting myself up for destroying all of my dreams and even my values. So, the list you have at this point is a way to be true to yourself and whoever you are going to spend the rest of your life with. It's about practicing honesty and not randomly going from one to another. Instead of feeling that you are not worthy enough to have the one you really want, tell yourself that you want to be true to yourself and honest in your relationship; this will help you overcome that feeling.

STEP 5

Feel it

I am sure after making your perfect list, everything will start happening for you and when it all finally comes together, you will have a beautiful story to share and inspire others. Now, as everything is working for you, you also need to sync yourself with the result you want to achieve. You need to create the feeling that you want to have when you are with your partner, the beautiful feeling of being unconditionally loved, being at peace, having fun, being supported, and the feeling of security around him/her.

There are many ways to nourish these feelings; one of the most effective one is meditation. I want you to create time for your relationship in your current life today. Spend a few minutes every day reading your list. Then, listen to relaxing music and imagine that you are with that person. Decide a scenario for the two of you like having a date, going to the beach, having a nice dinner, or simply going to buy groceries, buying clothes, cooking, celebrating your birthday, etc. Feel it as much as possible; how does that person smile? How does that person look at you with love? How does he/

she make you laugh? How does that person show he/she cares about you? Generate all these feelings in your mind as much as possible. If you have difficulty staying focused and thinking through, just write it down. But imagine as you write, feel it. Feel the security in your relationship, the peace, the happiness, the love.

Feeling is the key in this process! Coming back to me, I knew how I was feeling about my future husband. There was something special about the way he looked at me and his smile. It was the exact feeling and the exact look as with my husband today. It is not about the imaginary physical look I had in my head but the feeling I had when I was with that person during meditation.

Besides meditation, there were many scenarios in which I was feeling lonely and wished I had someone in my life. One of them was all those times I used to go buy groceries and see other couples. I would think I wish I had someone then. What I did was create an imaginary husband for myself. When I would be walking back with all the groceries in my hand, I would imagine him next to me, taking all of it from me or getting one of the bags to help me. I would think about that feeling, and it made me feel better. Funnily enough, it now happens and every time I go to the grocery shop with my husband. He carries everything, and every time he sees me carrying something he offers to help. It feels exactly the same as what I created that time and I am very very glad I did.

Another exercise is writing your story prior to it happening. I have a friend who has an amazing relationship with his wife. He told me that before they met, he used to write a book as his son talking about him and his lifestyle. Interestingly enough, his first child was a boy.

I used to have an app on my mobile for writing books on which I used to write about me and my husband. I had different chapters on how we met, our wedding, our love for each other, how we supported each other and so on. I would write it as a third person would write about us like my grandchildren.

Again, not everything I wrote turned out to be true but only the feeling. The feeling that was in those words is the feeling I have in my current relationship.

You can write about some scenarios here to generate initial feelings and then meditate on those feelings until they emerge:

1. Your first-year anniversary and your feeling in the last one year being with your dream person:

    ....
    ....
    ....
    ....
    ....
    ....

2. Shopping together:

    ....
    ....
    ....
    ....
    ....
    ....

3. A holiday together:

....
....
....
....
....
....

4. A very happy day with family or friends together

....
....
....
....
....
....

STEP 6

When bad things happen

If you started reading this book while having someone in your life, a broken relationship, or someone in particular that you wanted to be in your life, then read this chapter. Otherwise you can skip it.

You might have done everything right till this point while having someone in your mind and might have expected things to suddenly change for the better but things didn't go how you wanted and the relationship ended, leaving you feeling lost and confused. Or, you might meet someone and think this is the one but suddenly the relationship ends.

In my case, while I was doing everything and I was meditating and visualizing and feeling everything I wanted in a man, I had someone in my life who I really liked; he had most of the qualities I wanted but not all. Our relationship wasn't stable but it was improving, especially as I was doing the exercises I explained in the previous chapters. But suddenly, everything went wrong and we broke up. I was confused and needed clarification; the person I was dreaming to spend my life with left my side and now I was alone again, why? Fortunately, I was lucky enough to find a coach and during my call with her, she asked me many questions. Then she said that based on what I had done and the level of conversation I had with her, I had created something far more beautiful that I previously had. That the person I wanted had left for better. She was right, I was trying to compromise on what I really wanted with something similar, something that couldn't make my life better, couldn't make me happier, and couldn't fulfill my desires. But I was holding on to that because I was afraid of never finding anyone else closer to what I wanted, anyone better for me. I met my husband not long after that and I am so glad that relationship didn't get anywhere or I would have missed having my amazing husband in my life.

So in your case, if something suddenly changed in your life or if you had an unexpected break up that made you confused, don't doubt the energy and work that you put so far. You created something far more beautiful for you. Stay calm and everything would change for the better soon.

Also, if you think you wrote your list with someone you already know in your mind and not from your heart, now is the time to go back and revisit your list and do it again.

STEP 7

Dealing with stress

Doing everything in this book, sooner or later you will meet the one. You might be actively dating, or you might do nothing to meet that person in your life. You might feel that you can't do anything and just wait. You might be feeling nervous or feeling that nothing will happen and you will stay single forever. You might start going on different dating apps or visiting social events, trying to find someone. You might simply create a happy lifestyle that you enjoy with your current circumstances; just do what is more you!

All you need to do is keep calm and be at peace. Do the exercises in the previous chapters and only do things that make you happier from the inside. Avoid anything that does not resonate with you and not make you feel good. You also need to avoid anything that scares you or causes anxiety as it will only affect your mental and psychological health and might bring drama in your life and make your journey of finding true love longer.

Something you need to know is that the shortest path to your desire is your own happiness. There is something in this universe which some of us call God, some call the universe, and some call the collective mind. But there is something which is connected to everything and everybody and works based on the best of all. For now, I shall call it the 'Collective Mind.' The collective mind knows the shortest path for what you asked for and can show you the path the moment you ask. I hope this book is a part of that path that makes it even easier and faster for you to achieve what you want. It will show you the way and organize everything for you to the point that when you reflect, you will not believe how everything happened, how everything and everybody worked to make your wish come true. So, don't keep changing your goal every moment; stay focused. If in one minute you ask for your soulmate and a happy long-lasting relationship, someone to get old together with, but then change it to someone to fill your loneliness for the time being, then what do you think will happen? The one that you focus on most of the time always wins! That's the reason I want you to keep doing these exercises and spend your energy in something more rewarding than having temporary satisfaction. Do the work regardless of the direction you go; you will reach your destination faster by keeping your mind focused on your end goal.

Here are some real stories from real people and how they met their loved one after doing these exercises. Let's start with me. For a very long time I really wanted to learn tennis. I thought that maybe when I met the one, we can do it together but at the same time I knew there was something about it. I really wanted to learn tennis and had a very good feeling about it. I tried to find a coach and couldn't find any. I then searched the meetup and found only one group that was for the beginners with coaching included. I went there for the first time and met the coach who was very friendly and I also made some very good friends there. Then, the next few weeks my friends suggested having some private coaching sessions with that coach. They asked the coach to come and play with us once a week. Then my friend suggested asking him to join us for bowling. Then another friend suggested having dinner one night with that coach after tennis. Then the coach planned a short trip to the Australian Open with whoever wanted to come and before I knew it, the tennis coach asked me out and we started dating. All I did was join that group and everything else was because of my friends. His side of the story was the same. He had joined the group only two weeks before I joined because he wanted to have some fun somewhere very far from his working place; he wanted something for himself. He was also lonely and wanted to have someone special in his life. It so happened he had a good friend from his business who told him to make his list and made him think about the qualities he wanted. It was shortly after he wrote his list that he met me. He also hadn't had good relationships and wasn't dating. Funnily enough, he told about his interest in me to the organizer of that group and that person, knowing my culture and values, helped my husband and gave him tips to getting closer to me. He knew the entire time that I am the one. For me, on the other hand, it was like having a best friend who is kind and caring. Put it this way, I couldn't believe what was happening and couldn't trust it because it was the first time in my life that I was enjoying a non-dramatic and happy relationship with a man and didn't want to think about him as anything but a friend because I didn't want to destroy what I had, it was so good. But luckily, regardless of having all these thoughts and uncertainties, everything came together and everybody and everything helped both of us overcome all the challenges and so that we started dating each other.

Apart from my story, there is the story of another lady. She was going through a difficult time in her life and ended up having a small room with one of her friends and with a small child from her ex-husband. Being in a small town with not many people and other challenges, she had no hope to find anyone there. But through some amazing stories, her friend made her start developing a vision of a man with blue eyes and long hair who played the guitar. Her friend suggested they would need to leave the small town to meet this imaginary guy. She didn't want to follow her friend and leave town, but kept thinking of that guy and the feeling of happiness associated with him. One day, while she was at her job, cleaning the bar, a guy came in and asked her about a music group in town; he had come from another town to meet that group. This guy seemed to have all the characteristics she was looking for in a man. She said she didn't know but could ask around and let him know. Unfortunately, she couldn't find the information and called the guy to tell him. The guy said that it was fine and that if she didn't mind, he would like to have a coffee to thank her for her help. She went for coffee and the guy proposed to her; they married 19 days later! She was telling this story after 20 years of marriage.

There is another story of a girl who had planned to go for a trip she really wanted. However, the trip got cancelled and she was really upset. A friend of her asked her to join a party and even though she didn't want to go, her mother insisted that she should go instead of spending time being upset about something out of her control. She went to that party and met her man.

There was another lady who wasn't very outgoing; it so happened that a guy had a car crash near her house and funnily enough, they ended up getting married.

So, the point is that if you do what's best in your ability to create a good life for yourself, everything will come together to make your dream come true. Just create a healthy happy life with what you can and what is in your control, and the rest will follow. Make sure you do things that make you feel good because it means you are on the right path.

STEP 8

Knowledge of having a great relationship

Sooner or later, you will meet the one you imagined. But the question is, how much knowledge do you have about maintaining a good relationship? It's easy to start, but you need some basic knowledge to make it better and more joyful for both of you. How much do you know about the opposite sex regardless of what you have seen in movies and your daily interactions? How deep is your knowledge? I assume that none of us learned anything about relationships in school and not many of us have read books about it. All of our knowledge comes from the songs we relate to and the movies and TV shows we watch. However, none of them reflect reality because they all fall under the category of entertainment and their job is to keep you entertained without having any commitment to being real or correct. So, as you are doing exercises and doing meditations, spend time to read some basic books on marriage and relationships.

Here are some suggestions for you:

1. The Five Love Languages, by Gary Chapman. There is a book and there is a test.[2] So you can read the book and when you meet the loved one, you can ask them to do the test so you know about your partner's love language. The idea behind this book is that each one of us feels love differently. For one person love is when he/she receives a gift, for another person it can be a pat on the shoulder or hearing "I am so proud of you". So, this books makes it easier to know how the other person feels and what can make her/him loved.

2. Crucial Conversations, Tools for Talking When Stakes are High by Kerry Patterson, Joseph Grenny, Ron McMillan, and Al Switzler. This is one of the best books on the topic of interacting with others and improving the most difficult relationships in your professional and personal life. It has many examples of couples and how they can effectively interact with each other. You may not always agree on everything and you may not enjoy what the other one is doing. So how to convey your message in a respectful way? How to get the best outcome out of that conversation? You can find all the fundamentals, tips, and tricks in this book.

3. The Big Leap: Conquer Your Hidden Fear and Take Life to the Next Level by Gay Hendricks. This book will help you understand yourself better and overcome barriers to achieving your true potential and success in love and in life. There are times that everything is amazing, and you might have the best relationship ever on the entire planet. But if you are not conscious about your limits and the potential internal

---

[2] https://www.5lovelanguages.com/quizzes/

thermostat that you might have, then you might destroy it. So, this book will help you overcome your limits and be prepared for a better life.

4. Guide to Getting It on by Paul Joannides. This book is an instructional book about sex. It is fun to read and very informative. It covers every topic a couple could possibly be curious about. It gives very good information about body and pleasure and understanding the opposite sex.

5. The Magic by Rhonda Byrne. This book will really make a difference to your life if you do the practices daily and especially if you continue after the book has finished. The Magic is about being grateful in life and attracting more goodness by appreciating what you have today. If you are not in a good state and have depression or if you don't enjoy your life and are having difficulty changing it, then this can be a good start for you.

6. The Six Pillars of Self-Esteem by Nathaniel Branden. Some people find this book life changing while others find it hard to understand. But there is a YouTube[3] video that explains it and you can see if it's the book you need to read or not. This book helps you be more confident, more reliable, and more accountable.

---

[3]   https://youtu.be/dhuabY4DmEo

STEP 9

Daily routine

Here is a suggested daily routine you can have according to the exercises you have read in this book. Depending on your schedule you might change it, but it is important to allocate time and space in your life for a nice relationship.

	MON	TUE	WED	THU	FRI	SAT	SUN
WEEK1	Meditation & mirror practice	Treat yourself	Meditation & mirror practice	Read one of the suggested books	Meditation & mirror practice	Do something fun	Meditation & mirror practice & Catch up with someone
WEEK2	Meditation & mirror practice	Treat yourself	Meditation & mirror practice	Read one of the suggested books	Meditation & mirror practice	Do something you love	Meditation & mirror practice
WEEK3	Meditation & mirror practice	Treat yourself	Meditation & mirror practice	Read one of the suggested books	Meditation & mirror practice	Do something fun	Meditation & mirror practice & Catch up with someone
WEEK4	Meditation & mirror practice	Treat yourself	Meditation & mirror practice	Read one of the suggested books	Meditation & mirror practice	Do something you love	Meditation & mirror practice

STEP 10

Stay connected

I would love to hear your love story after reading this book. Feel free to write your story in a personal email or on my Facebook page. Try to stay connected and get inspired by other amazing stories because it will strengthen your belief that if others have it, then you can have it too.

I have created a page called THE PLANET LOVE on Facebook which you can join and where you can contribute to create a planet full of loving relationships and beautiful happy families. It doesn't matter if you don't feel this way right now. The fact that you have read this book so far indicates that you have a desire to have one. If there is desire there is a way. Whoever gave you the dream can bring it to pass. Everyone is born single and has experienced what you might be experiencing at this point. Just stay connected and later you can share your story with the world to inspire others and create a more loving place and happier families on earth.

You can also write an email to me with your story and I can post it on your behalf as anonymous.

Facebook page: theplanetlove
Email: info.theplanetlove@gmail.com

There is another exercise that will help you stay connected offline. This exercise is called Mind Movies[4]. Mind Movies is a company owned by Natalie Ledwith. In this exercise you create your own movie of what you think you want to experience, let us say within the next 5 years. You find some photos that resonate with what you want to experience and create a slideshow. You then add music to the background of the slideshow and play it every day. The length of the slide show should be around 5mins.

The idea is to "change the way you feel, then you will change the way you think, which changes the way you act resulting in what you will achieve". When you build the movie you activate the cerebellum, which in turn switches off the thinking part of the brain, bypassing the analytical mind. Then you reach a state of single-minded thought and creativity.

You can use her instructions and her pre-made movies or you can create your own. It is similar to having a vision board but more effective as it involves more of your senses and evokes deeper feelings. You can find positive affirmations, inspiring images, and motivating music and can create a movie or a slideshow which you can watch every day. It will keep your brain in the manifestation mode for a longer time. It's better to keep it between 3–5 minutes long and not more as you lose your focus after 5 minutes.

---

[4]   https://www.mindmovies.com/mm4/index.php
       https://www.mindmovies.com/index.php

I had both a vision board and a mind movie. With my vision board, I printed some nice photos of the different aspects of my life, photos that resonate with me and what I want to experience in my life. I then wrote a few words next to the photos; words that would remind me of my feelings attached with them the next time I looked at them. Words like, 'peace', 'true love', 'joy', 'happiness', 'fun', etc. Then I used these photos and added some sentences on what I wanted to experience with music and created my mind movie which was technically a slideshow with music. I watched it for some time.

What I can say is that a few years after I had done this exercise, I experienced similar events in my life that I had on my board and in the movie. The feeling I had in these events was the same that what I wanted in my vision board and movie. Not everything on my list has happened yet, as I created the movie for the next 5 years of my life and still have some time to go. But I think it's worth creating such a board or movie to accelerate the process of achieving your dreams and staying connected with what you really want in your life.

CPSIA information can be obtained
at www.ICGtesting.com
Printed in the USA
BVHW031938031120
592440BV00009B/68